Copyright © 2006 by Robert W. Pelton

ISBN 0-7414-3623-X

Published by:

INFINITY
PUBLISHING.COM

1094 New DeHaven Street, Suite 100
West Conshohocken, PA 19428-2713
Info@buybooksontheweb.com
www.buybooksontheweb.com
Toll-free (877) BUY BOOK
Local Phone (610) 941-9999
Fax (610) 941-9959

Printed in the United States of America

Printed on Recycled Paper

Published October 2007

George Washington' Prophetic Vision

A Uniquely Different Piece of American History

Made from an impression of George Washington's face while he was still alive. It is in all probability the most accurate likeness of Washington ever made.

FOREWORD

The winter at Valley Forge was bitter cold. The Continental Army under General George Washington had little food, inadequate shelter, and insufficient clothing. Many soldiers had no boots – their bloody feet were wrapped in rags. Often there was no pay. Sickness ravaged the camp. Before spring, more than one third of the men would die of disease or desert the cause. All odds were against them....

The General gathered his weary troops around him on Christmas Eve and read them the inspiring immortal words of Thomas Paine: *"These are the times that try men's souls. The summer soldier and the sunshine patriot will, in this crisis, shrink from the service of their country: but he that stands it now, deserves the love and thanks of man and woman. Tyranny, like hell, is not easily conquered; yet we have this consolation with us, that the harder the conflict, the more glorious the triumph. What we obtain too cheap, we esteem too lightly: it is dearness only that gives everything its value. Heaven knows how to put a proper price upon goods; and it would be strange indeed if so celestial an article as freedom should not be so highly rated".*

John Grady, M.D., Benton, Tennessee

Encouraged by the deeply moving words of Paine, strengthened by the leadership and determination of Washington, and confident in the providence of God; the loyal men at Valley Forge assembled, crossed -the icy Delaware River, and won the battle of Trenton – the turning point in the Revolutionary War.

Part of the Pelton Historical Book Series

Includes the Following Titles:

George Washington: God's Chosen Leader

George Washington's Prophetic Vision

Man of Destiny: George Washington

Men of Destiny – Signers of Our Declaration of Independence & Our Constitution

America: A Christian Nation? Here Are the Facts!

Baking Recipes from the Wives and Mothers of Our Founding Fathers

Cooking Recipes from the Wives and Mothers of Our Founding Fathers

Baking Recipes from the Wives and Mothers of Civil War Heroes, Heroines & Other Notables

Historical Thanksgiving Cookery

Historical Christmas Cookery

Civil War Period Cookery

Revolutionary War Period Cookery

Dedication

To my early descendants, Barnabus Horton of Leicestershire, England, who sailed to America on the *Swallow* some time between 1633 and 1638 with his wife Mary and their two sons, Joseph and Benjamin. They landed at Hampton, Massachusetts, and were Puritans.

And also to my Great great-grandmother Huldah Radike Horton, one of the finest and most famous horsewomen of her day. She had the honor of entertaining Lafayette in her home and riding at his side in a parade in his honor in Newburg, New York, in 1824. The French General and friend of the young Republic was making his second and final visit.

CONTENTS

1

Meet the Real
George Washington

President of the Constitutional Convention

Washington as well as every man who signed the *Declaration of Independence* bravely refused an offer of amnesty from British Governor Gage in June of 1775. Each man well knew that he was risking losing everything, including his life. That should the struggle for Independence fail, an ignominious death by hanging would most certainly be his punishment.

Washington, suffered heavy monetary losses because of his connection with the cause. Much of his extensive fortune was lost due to financial sacrifices and long absences during the war.

Many Signers of the *Declaration of Independence* suffered much more dire punishments. Here are but a few examples:

John Hart: His home was pillaged and then burned it to the ground. Following a scorched earth policy, the vengeful British destroyed his livestock and laid waste to his land. His wife lay dying while his 13 children fled to the  woods. Hart was hunted down like an animal and forced to live in caves for more than a year. Finally able to return home only to find that his entire family had vanished. Hart died a few weeks later of a broken heart.

 **Richard Stockton:** Captured by the British and held in prison. Severely beaten and starved in an attempt to force him to betray his country and his friends. His estate was pillaged, plundered and burned. Crops were wantonly destroyed, cattle and horses either stolen or killed. He ended up a destitute man, a beggar.

Abraham Clark: Both sons were captured and treated with exceptional brutality because their father had signed the *Declaration*. Both were incarcerated on the *Jersey*, a notorious, infamous, disease-ridden British prison ship.

Despite the fact that every man knew his possible fate, not one became a turncoat! Not one took Gage's offer! In fact, each man was unwavering and most courageous.

Yet this great American patriot didn't have the honor of signing the *Declaration of Independence*. He certainly would have done so had the opportunity presented itself. Then why did he not sign the grand document?

George Washington was not in attendance at the *Continental Congress* when the *Declaration* was signed. He was at the time Commander-in Chief of the Continental Army and far away serving in this capacity.

Regarding George Washington, John Grady, a physician and former United States Navy jet pilot has this to say: *"Because of the devotion and vision of one man, and the loyalty and courage of a small force of fighting Americans – the course of history was forever changed."*

And so it was!

The *Declaration of Independence* is the most important of all American historical documents. It is essentially a partisan document, a justification of the American Revolution presented to the world. Its unique combination of general principles and an abstract theory of government with a detailed enumeration of specific grievances and injustices has given it enduring power as one of the great political documents of the West.

George Washington presided over the Constitutional Convention, during which time the *Constitution* was approved and adopted at the State house in Philadelphia on September 17, 1787. Only he, a moral, honorable and dignified man – through personal example, committed leadership and force of character – could hold the strong-willed, opinion-differing men together at the glorious *Constitutional Convention*. The destiny of a great nation lay upon the shoulders of this fearless heroic leader.

Hall of Heroes

Inducted by *Life Magazine* in 1998 into its **Hall of Heroes**, these words most appropriately written by historian Garry Wills: *"Washington is the greatest President, greatest leader, greatest politician. He steered a course through revolution and nation-building with immense tact and wisdom. Nobody else could have done it."*

He was equal to the task.

This man was the personification of the uppermost inherent worth of Western man.

He was a man of understanding, judgment, and devotion to and faith in God.

He was a solider of physical strength, uprightness, and moral fiber beyond reproach.

He was a Christian patriot with a sense of destiny and great courage.

He was willing to fight and die for a just cause, his cause.

An American Hero

Yes, George Washington is an American hero whose eminence is not fully covered by the record of his life. For example, the man was substantially greater than anything he did.

He was a military genius, a mastermind.

He wrenched freedom, independence and liberty from oppression.

He was an outstanding statesman.

He helped evolve a secure government from political turmoil.

He was a patriot.

He refused a crown.

Wisdom and understanding, persistence, forbearance, bravery, dedication to the worthy cause animated his every act.

Thanklessness, unfairness and disloyalty never disillusioned him, but served to reinforce and make his character stronger.

He grew in dignity and in capability to the need of his mounting responsibility and authority.

He never became pompous or disdainful.

Personal aspirations and selfish opportunity never tempted him from the slender corridor of honor.

After his second term expired, Washington again retired to civilian life. He thereby established an important precedent of peaceful change of government that was to serve as an example for the United States and for future Republics throughout the world.

Because of his central role in the founding of the United States, Washington is often called the *"Father of the Country."* Scholars rank him among the greatest of United States presidents.

A British Leader's Comment

Yes, this is the man who was so highly honored by the great British statesman and four times Prime Minister, William Gladstone.

Gladstone once proposed the creation of a grouping of pedestals for statues of history's greatest men.

The pedestal in the center was noticeably higher that the others.

Gladstone was asked to identify the figure to be given the place of honor on the highest pedestal.

Without hesitating, he answered: *"George Washington."*

This just about says it all!

2

Washington's Adopted Daughter Writes About Her Father

Eleanor (Nelly) Parke Custis Lewis wrote the letter to follow to Jared Sparks, an author who was at the time compiling a book of the writings of George Washington. He had asked her for information on the religious beliefs of the man who had adopted her. The book was later published as *"The Life of Washington "*

"Woodlawn, 26 February, 1833.

"Sir,

"I received your favor of the 20th instant last evening, and hasten to give you the information, which you desire.

"Truro Parish is the one in which Mount Vernon, Pohick Church, and Woodlawn are situated. Fairfax Parish is now Alexandria. Before the Federal District was ceded to Congress, Alexandria was in Fairfax County. General Washington had a pew in Pohick Church, and one in Christ Church at Alexandria. He was very instrumental in establishing Pohick Church, and I believe subscribed largely. His pew was near the pulpit. I have a perfect recollection of being there, before his election to the presidency, with him and my grandmother. It was a beautiful church, and had a large, respectable, and wealthy congregation, who were regular attendants.

"He attended the church at Alexandria, when the weather and roads permitted a ride of ten miles. In New York and Philadelphia he never omitted attendance at church in the morning, unless detained by indisposition. The afternoon was spent in his own room at home; the evening with his family, and without company. Sometimes an old and intimate friend called to see us for an hour or two; but visiting and visitors were prohibited for that day.

"No one in church attended to the services with more reverential respect. My grandmother, who was eminently pious, never deviated from her early habits. She always knelt. The General, as was then the custom, stood during the devotional parts of the service. On communion Sundays, he left the church with me, after the blessing, and returned home, and we sent the carriage back for my grandmother.

"It was his custom to retire to his library at nine or ten o'clock, where he remained an hour before he went to his chamber. He always rose before the sun, and remained in his library until called to breakfasdt [sic]. I never witnessed his private devotions. I never inquired about them. I should have thought it the greatest heresy to doubt his firm belief in Christianity. His life, his writings, prove that he was a Christian. He was not one of those who act or pray, "that they may be seen of men." He communed with his God in secret.

"My mother resided two years at Mount Vernon, after her marriage with John Parke Custis, the only son of Mrs. Washington. I have heard her say that General Washington always received the sacrament with my grandmother before the revolution. When my aunt, Miss Custis, died suddenly at Mount Vernon, before they could realize the event, he knelt by her and prayed most fervently, most affectingly, for her recovery. Of this I was assured by Judge Washington's mother, and other witnesses.

"He was a silent, thoughtful man. He spoke little generally; never of himself. I never heard him relate a single act of his life during the war. I have often seen him perfectly abstracted, his lips moving, but no sound was perceptible. I have sometimes made him laugh most heartily from sympathy with my joyous and extravagant spirits. I was probably one of the last persons on earth to whom he would have addressed serious conversation, particularly when he knew that I had the most perfect model of female excellence ever with me as my monitress, who acted the part of a tender and devoted parent, loving me as only a mother can love, and never extenuating or approving in me what she disapproved in others.

"She never omitted her private devotions, or her public duties; and she and her husband were so perfectly united and happy, that he must have been a Christian. She had no doubts, no fears for him. After forty years of devoted affection and uninterrupted happiness, she resigned him without a murmur into the arms of his Savior and his God, with the assured hope of his eternal felicity. Is it necessary that any one should certify, "General Washington avowed himself to me a believer in Christianity?" As well may we question his patriotism, his heroic, disinterested devotion to his country. His mottos were, *'Deeds, not Words'*; and, *'For God and my Country.'*

"With sentiments of esteem, I am, & c."

3

A Man of Much Reverence and Prayer

Washington's Faith in God

Washington, *"without making ostentatious professions of religion, was a sincere believer in the Christian faith, and a truly devout man,"* according to John Marshall, first Chief Justice of the United States Supreme Court. Marshall had fought with General Washington at Valley Forge during the War for Independence.

After Washington died on December 4, 1799, Reverend J. T. Kirkland said: *"The virtues of our departed friend were crowned by piety. He is known to have been habitually devout. To Christian institutions he gave the countenance of his, example; and no one could express, more fully, his sense of the Providence of God, and the dependence of man."*

His Spiritual Life

Washington dutifully recorded the words of advice his mother, Mary, gave him when he was leaving home to begin what would turn out to be a lifelong service to his country. She said: *"Remember that God is our only one trust. To Him, I commend you ... My son, neglect not the duty of secret prayer."*

Throughout his life, whether while a young man, Commander-in-Chief of the Continental Army, or President of the United States, George Washington would promptly stand up at exactly

9:00 pm, take his candle, and go off by himself. There, from 9:00pm to 10:00pm, he wouldn't be seen. He was alone on his knees in front of a chair praying. A candle stood on a stand next to the chair. And his *Bible* was open before him. This he would do even when guests were present. Then promptly at 10:00pm, he would emerge and go directly to his bedroom.

He'd get up every morning at 4:00am, and spend another hour in the same room. He could be found kneeling before the same chair, in the same posture, with the same *Bible* open before him.

William White comments on the personal life of Washington's in his book, **Washington's Writing**: *"It seems proper to subjoin to this letter what was told to me by Mr. Robert Lewis, at Fredericksburg, in the year 1827. Being a nephew of Washington, and his private secretary during the first part of his presidency, Mr. Lewis lived with him on terms of intimacy, and had the best opportunity for observing his habits.*

"Mr. Lewis said that he had accidentally witnessed his private devotions in his library both morning and evening; that on those occasions he had seen him in a kneeling posture with a Bible open before him, and that he believed such to have been his daily practice."

Washington made a practice of never traveling unnecessarily on the Sabbath. He never, no matter what the circumstances, received visitors on Sunday, with one exception, a Godly friend named Trumbel. They would spend time reading the **Bible** and praying together.

Henry Muhlenberg was the pastor of the Lutheran church near Valley Forge. He also was one of the founders of the Lutheran Church in America. He said this about Washington while he was in command of the Continental Army: *"I heard a fine example today, namely, that His Excellency General Washington rode around among his army yesterday and admonished each and every one to fear God, to put away the wickedness that has set in and become so general, and to practice the Christian virtues. From all appearances, this gentleman does not belong to the so-called world of society, for he respects God's Word, believes in the atonement through Christ, and bears himself in humility and gentleness. Therefore, the Lord God has also singularly, yea, marvelously, preserved him from harm in the midst of countless perils, ambuscades, fatigues, etc., and has hitherto graciously held him in His hand as a chosen vessel."*

Washington's Oath and Actions

When Washington took his oath of office as President of the United States, he subsequently bent forward and kissed the **Bible** on which he had just taken his oath.

The *Bible* was opened to the **Book of Genesis.**

He then led the Senate and the House of Representatives to the church for a two hour worship service.

"The people know," said George Washington, *"it is impossible to rightly govern the world with out God and the Bible."*

References to God

Used more than 80 different names in reference to God in his prayers and his writings. They included:

Almighty Being

All Wise Dispenser of Events

Beneficent Author of the Universe

The God of Armies

Author of All Good

Eternal Lord God

Most Gracious God

Thy Divine Majesty

King of Heaven

Washington's Prayer Plaque

Washington's Prayer has been preserved for posterity on the plaque at Pohick Church in Fairfax, Virginia. Washington was a vestryman there from 1762 to 1784. It is also to be found on a plaque in New York City's St. Paul's Chapel:

"Almighty God; We make our earnest prayer that Thou wilt keep the United States in Thy Holy protection; and Thou wilt incline the hearts of the Citizens to cultivate a spirit of subordination and obedience to Government; and entertain a brotherly affection and love for one(another and for their fellow Citizens of the United States at large, and particularly for their brethren who have served in the Field.

"And finally that Thou wilt most graciously be pleased to dispose us all to do justice, to love mercy, and to demean ourselves with that Charity, humility, and pacific temper of mind which were the Characteristics of the Divine Author of our blessed Religion, and without a humble imitation of whose example in these things we can never hope to be a happy nation.

"Grant our supplication, we beseech Thee, through Jesus Christ our Lord. Amen.

The Inscription on Washington's Tomb

This inscription is engraved above Washington's tomb. It was taken from the Book of John, Chapter 11, Verses 25-26:

"I am the Resurrection and the Life; saith the Lord. He that believeth in Me, though he were dead yet shall he live. And whosoever liveth and believeth in Me shall never die."

The Washington Monument

The beautiful and towering Washington Monument in Washington, D.C., stands over 555 feet high. These words, befitting the Founder of our country, are engraved on the metal cap: **"Praise be to God"**.

The following prayers are those found in George Washington's personal field notebook. There were a total of 24 pages, each of which was written by this great man. They certainly reveal the depth of his character.

1) Sunday Morning

Almighty God, and most merciful Father, who didst command the children of Israel to offer a daily sacrifice to thee, that thereby they might glorify and praise thee for thy protection both night and day, receive, O Lord, my morning sacrifice which I now offer up to thee; I yield thee humble and hearty thanks that thou has preserved me from the danger of the night past, and brought me to the light of the day, and the comforts thereof, a day which is consecrated to Thine own service and for thine own honor. Let my heart, therefore, Gracious God, be so affected with the glory and majesty of it, that I may not do mine own works, but wait on thee, and discharge those weighty duties thou requirest of me, and since thou art a God of pure eyes, and wilt be sanctified in all who draw near unto thee, who doest not regard the sacrifice of fools, nor hear sinners who tread in thy courts, pardon, I beseech thee, my sins, remove them from thy presence, as far as the east is from the west, and accept of me for the merits of thy son Jesus Christ, that when I come into thy temple, and compass thine altar, my prayers may come before thee as incense; and as thou wouldst hear me calling upon thee in my prayers, so give me grace to hear thee calling on me in thy word, that it may be wisdom, righteousness, reconciliation and peace to the saving of the soul in the day of the Lord Jesus. Grant that I may hear it with reverence, receive it with meekness, mingle it with faith, and that it may accomplish in me, Gracious God, the good work for which thou has sent it. Bless my family, kindred, friends and country, be our God & guide this day and for ever for his sake, who ay down in the Grave and arose again for us, Jesus Christ our Lord, Amen.

(2) Sunday Evening

O most Glorious God, in Jesus Christ my merciful and loving father, I acknowledge and confess my guilt, in the weak and imperfect performance of the duties of this day. I have called on thee for pardon and forgiveness of sins, but so coldly and carelessly, that my prayers are become my sin and stand in need of pardon. I have heard thy holy word, but with such deadness of spirit that I have been an unprofitable and forgetful hearer, so that, O Lord, tho' I have done thy work, yet it hath been so negligently that I may rather expect a curse than a blessing from thee. But, O God, who art rich in mercy and plenteous in redemption, mark not, I beseech thee, what I have done amiss; remember that I am but dust, and remit my transgressions, negligences & ignorances, and cover them all with the absolute obedience of thy dear Son, that those sacrifices which I have offered may be accepted by thee, in and for the sacrifice of Jesus Christ offered upon the cross for me; for his sake, ease me of the burden of my sins, and give me grace that by the call of the Gospel I may rise from the slumber of sin into the newness of life. Let me live according to those holy rules which thou hast this day prescribed in thy holy word; make me to know what is acceptable in thy holy word; make me to know what is acceptable in thy sight, and therein to delight, open the eyes of my understanding, and help me thoroughly to examine myself concerning my knowledge, faith and repentance, increase my faith, and direct me to the true object Jesus Christ the way, the truth and the life, bless O Lord, all the people of this land, from the highest to the lowest, particularly those whom thou has appointed to rule over us in church & state. continue thy goodness to me this night. These weak petitions I humbly implore thee to hear accept and ans. for the sake of thy Dear Son Jesus Christ our Lord, Amen.

(3) Monday Morning

O eternal and everlasting God, I presume to present myself this morning before thy Divine majesty, beseeching thee to accept of my humble and hearty thanks, that it hath pleased thy great goodness to keep and preserve me the night past from all the dangers poor mortals are subject to, and has given me sweet and pleasant sleep, whereby I find my body refreshed and comforted for performing the duties of this day, in which I beseech thee to defend me from all perils of body and soul. Direct my thoughts, words and work, wash away my sins in the immaculate blood of the lamb, and purge my heart by thy holy spirit, from the dross of my natural corruption, that I may with more freedom of mind and liberty of will serve thee, the ever lasting God, in righteousness and holiness this day, and all the days of my life. Increase my faith in the sweet promises of the gospel; give me repentance from dead works; pardon my wanderings, & direct my thoughts unto

thyself, the God of my salvation; teach me how to live in thy fear, labor in thy service, and ever to run in the ways of thy commandments; make me always watchful over my heart, that neither the terrors of conscience, the loathing of holy duties, the love of sin, nor an unwillingness to depart this life, may cast me into a spiritual slumber, but daily frame me more 7 more into the likeness of thy son Jesus Christ, that living in thy fear, and dying in thy favor, I may in thy appointed time attain the resurrection of the just unto eternal life bless my family, friends & kindred unite us all in praising & glorifying thee in all our works begun, continued, and ended, when we shall come to make our last account before thee blessed savior, who hath taught us thus to pray, our Father, & c.

(4) Monday Evening

Most Gracious Lord God, from whom proceedeth every good and perfect gift, I offer to thy divine majesty my unfeigned praise & thanksgiving for all thy mercies towards me. Thou mad'st me at first and hast ever since sustained the work of thy own hand; thou gav'st thy Son to die for me; and hast given me assurance of salvation, upon my repentance and sincerely endeavoring to conform my life to his holy precepts and example. Thou art pleased to lengthen out to me the time of repentance and to move me to it by thy spirit and by the word, by thy mercies, and by thy judgments; out of a deepness of thy mercies, and by my own unworthiness, I do appear before thee at this time; I have sinned and done very wickedly, be merciful to me, O God, and pardon me for Jesus Christ sake; instruct me in the particulars of my duty, and suffer me not to be tempted above what thou givest me strength to bear. Take care, I pray thee of my affairs and more and more direct me in thy truth, defend me from my enemies, especially my spiritual ones. Suffer me not to be drawn from thee, by the blandishments of the world, carnal desires, the cunning of the devil, or deceitfulness of sin. work in me thy good will and pleasure, and discharge my mind from all things that are displeasing to thee, of all ill will and discontent, wrath and bitterness, pride & vain conceit of myself, and render me charitable, pure, holy, patient and heavenly minded. be with me at the hour of death; dispose me for it, and deliver me from the slavish fear of it, and make me willing and fit to die whenever thou shalt call me hence. Bless our rulers in church and state. bless O Lord the whole race of mankind, and let the world be filled with the knowledge of Thee and thy son Jesus Christ. Pity the sick, the poor, the weak, the needy, the widows and fatherless, and all that morn or are broken in heart, and be merciful to them according to their several necessities. bless my friends and grant me grace to forgive my enemies as heartily as I desire forgiveness of Thee my heavenly Father. I beseech thee to defend me this night from all evil, and do more for me than I can think or ask, for Jesus Christ sake, in whose most holy name & words, I continue to pray, Our Father, & c.

(5) Tuesday Morning

O Lord our God, most mighty and merciful father, I thine unworthy creature and servant, do once more approach thy presence. Though not worthy to appear before thee, because of my natural corruptions, and the many sins and transgressions which I have committed against thy divine majesty; yet I beseech thee, for the sake of him in whom thou art well pleased, the Lord Jesus Christ, to admit me to render thee deserved thanks and praises for thy manifold mercies extended toward me, for the quiet rest & repose of the past night, for food, rainment, health, peace, liberty, and the hopes of a better life through the merits of thy dear son's bitter passion. and O kind father continue thy mercy and favor to me this day, and ever hereafter; propose all my lawful undertakings; et me have all my directions from thy holy spirit; and success from thy bountiful hand. Let the bright beams of thy light so shine into my heart, and enlighten my mind in understanding thy blessed word, that I may be enabled to perform thy will in all things, and effectually resist all temptations of the world, the flesh and the devil.

preserve and defend our rulers in church & state. bless the people of this land, be a father to the fatherless, a comforter to the comfortless, a deliverer to the captives, and a physician to the sick. Let thy blessings guide this day and forever through J. C. in whose blessed form of prayer I conclude my weak petitions--Our Father, & c.

(6) Tuesday Evening

Most gracious God and heavenly father, we cannot cease, but must cry unto thee for mercy, because my sins cry against me for justice. How shall I address myself unto thee, I must with the publican stand and admire at thy great goodness, tender mercy, and long suffering towards me, in that thou hast kept me the past day from being consumed and brought to naught. O Lord, what is man, or the son of man, that thou regardest him; the more days pass over my head, the more sins and iniquities I heap up against thee. If I should cast up the account of my good deeds done this day, how few and small would they be; but if I should reckon my miscarriages, surely they would be many and great. O, blessed father, let thy son's blood wash me from all impurities, and cleanse me from the stains of sin that are upon me. Give me grace to lay hold upon his merits; that they may be my reconciliation and atonement unto thee,--That I may know my sins are forgiven by his death & passion. embrace me in the arms of thy mercy; vouchsafe to receive me unto the bosom of thy love, shadow me with thy wings, that I may safely rest under thy suspicion this night; and so into thy hands I commend myself, both soul and body, in the name of thy son, J. C., beseeching Thee, when this life shall end, I may take my everlasting rest with thee in thy heavenly kingdom. bless all in authority over us, be merciful to all those afflicted with thy cross or calamity, bless all my friends, forgive my enemies and accept my thanksgiving this evening for all the mercies and favors afforded me; hear and graciously answer these my requests, and whatever else thou see'st needful grant us, for the sake of Jesus Christ in whose blessed name and words I continue to pray, Our Father, & c.

(7) A Prayer for Wednesday Morning

Almighty and eternal Lord God, the great creator of heaven & earth, and the God and Father of our Lord Jesus Christ; look down from heaven, in pity and compassion upon me thy servant, who humbly prostrate myself before thee, sensible of thy mercy and my own misery; there is an infinite distance between thy glorious majesty and me, thy poor creature, the work of thy hand, between thy infinite power, and my weakness, thy wisdom, and my folly, thy eternal Being, and my mortal frame, but, O Lord, I have set myself at a greater distance from thee by my sin and wickedness, and humbly acknowledge the corruption of my nature and the many rebellions of my life. I have sinned against heaven and before thee, in thought, word & deed; I have contemned thy majesty and holy laws. I have likewise sinned by omitting what I ought to do, and committing what I ought not. I have rebelled against light, despised thy mercies and judgments, and broken my vows and promises; I have neglected the means of Grace, and opportunities of becoming better; my iniquities are multiplies, and my sins are very great. I confess them, O Lord, with shame and sorrow, detestation and loathing, and desire to be vile in my own eyes, as I have rendered myself vile in thine. I humbly beseech thee to be merciful to me in the free pardon of my sins, for the sake of thy dear Son, my only savior, J. C., who came not to call the righteous, but sinners to repentance; be pleased to renew my nature and write thy laws upon my heart, and help me to live, righteously, soberly, and godly in this evil worlds; make me humble, meek, patient and contented, and work in me the grace of thy holy spirit. Prepare me for death and judgment, and let the thoughts thereof awaken me to a greater care and study to approve myself unto thee in well doing. bless our rulers in church & state. Help all in affliction or adversity--give them patience and a sanctified use of their affliction, and in thy good time deliverance from them; forgive my enemies, take me unto thy protection this day, keep me in perfect peace, which I ask in the name & for the sake of Jesus. Amen.

(8) Wednesday Evening

Holy and eternal Lord God who art the King of heaven, and the watchman of Israel, that never slumberest or sleepest, what shall we render unto thee for all thy benefits; because thou hast inclined thine ears unto me, therefore will I call on thee as long as I live, from the rising of the sun to the going down of the same let thy name be praised. among the infinite riches of thy mercy towards me, I desire to render thanks & praise for thy merciful preservation of me this day, as well as all the days of my life; and for the many other blessings & mercies spiritual & temporal which thou hast bestowed on me, contrary to my deserving. All these thy mercies call on me to be thankful and my infirmities & wants call for a continuance of thy tender mercies; cleanse my soul, O Lord, I beseech thee, from whatever is offensive to thee, and hurtful to me, and give me what is convenient for me. watch over me this night, and give me comfortable and sweet sleep to fit me for the service of the day following. Let my soul watch for the coming of the Lord Jesus; let my bed put me in mind of my grave, and my rising from there of my last resurrection; O heavenly Father, so frame this heart of mine, that I may ever delight to live according to thy will and command, in holiness and righteousness before thee all the days of my life. Let me remember, O Lord, the time will come when the trumpet shall sound, and the dead shall rise and stand before the judgment seat, and give an account of whatever they have done in the body, and let me so prepare my soul, that I may do it with joy and not with grief. bless the rulers and people of this and forget not those who are under any affliction or oppression.

Let thy favor be extended to all my relations friends and all others who I ought to remember in my prayer and hear me I beseech thee for the sake of my dear redeemer in whose most holy words, I farther pray, Our Father, & c.

(9) Thursday Morning

Most gracious Lord God, whose dwelling is in the highest heavens, and yet beholdest the lowly and humble upon the earth, I blush and am ashamed to lift up my eyes to thy dwelling place, because I have sinned against thee; look down, I beseech thee upon me thy unworthy servant who prostrate myself at the footstool of thy mercy, confessing my own guiltiness, and begging pardon for my sins; what couldst thou have done Lord more for me, or what could I have done more against thee? Thou didst send me thy Son to take nature upon.

NOTE: The prayer book ended on this page. Were the rest of Washington's prayer pages lost? Or did he not complete his prayer list? This has never been determined.

Washington's Prayer on May 1, 1777, when he received the news that France was joining the Colonies in the War for American Independence:

"And now, Almighty Father, if it is Thy holy will that we shall obtain a place and name among the nations of the earth, grant that we may be enabled to show our gratitude for Thy goodness by our endeavors to fear and obey Thee. Bless us with Thy wisdom in our counsels, success in battle, and let all our victories be tempered with humanity. Endow, also, our enemies with enlightened minds, that they become sensible of their injustice, and willing to restore our liberty and peace. Grant the petition of Thy servant, for the sake of Him whom Thou hast called Thy beloved Son; nevertheless, not my will, but Thine be done.

Praying at Valley Forge

The famed painting of George Washington kneeling in prayer in the snow-covered woods of Valley Forge is based on fact. We have all probably heard of his prayer that was overheard by a Quaker, a pacifist, a Tory – a man loyal to the Crown. This man returned home shaken and told his wife: *"Our cause is lost! I came unexpectedly in the woods upon a man who was kneeling in prayer. As I drew closer, I heard his voice. I heard the impassioned plea of his prayers and saw the tears on his cheeks. I knew our cause was lost."*

The Quaker and his wife were so overwhelmed that they became supporters of Washington and the American quest for Independence cause.

A slightly different version of this same story comes from William J. Fedder's **America's God and Country**:

"In 1777 while the American army lay at Valley Forge, a good old Quaker by the name of Potts had occasion to pass through a thick woods near headquarters. As he traversed the dark brown forest, he heard, at a distance before him, a voice which as he advanced became more fervid....

"Approaching with slowness and circumspection, whom should he behold in a dark bower, apparently formed for the purpose, but the

Commander-in-Chief of the armies of the United Colonies on his knees in the act of devotion to the Ruler of the Universe!

"At the moment when Friend Potts, concealed by the trees, came up, Washington was interceding for his beloved country. With tones of gratitude that labored for adequate expression he

adored that exuberant goodness which, from the depth of obscurity, had exalted him to the head of a great nation, and that nation fighting at fearful odds for all the world holds dear.

"Soon as the General had finished his devotions and had retired, Friend Potts returned to his house, and threw himself into a chair by the side of his wife. 'Heigh! Isaac!' said she with tenderness, 'thee seems agitated; what's the matter?'

"'Indeed, my dear' quoth he, 'if I appear agitated 'tis no more than what I have seen this day what I shall never forget. Till now I have bought that a Christian and a soldier were characters incompatible; but if George Washington be not a man of God, l am mistaken, and still more shall I be disappointed if God does not through him perform some great thing for this country.'"

4

George Washington's
Prophetic Vision

Washington's Headquarters at Valley Forge where the "vision" is said to have taken place.

A Momentous Event at Valley Forge

One of the most telling events in the life of this *Man of Destiny* will not be found in any of our high school or college history texts. But it certainly should be!

It is said to have taken place during the dread winter of 1777. This was a time when the Revolutionary War wasn't going well for the vastly outnumbered and ill-equipped Colonial forces.

The Continental Army had been defeated in two major battles and British invaders occupied Philadelphia!

Washington had retreated to the Pennsylvania plains.

The situation was desperate!

There was near famine!

Temperatures fell far below zero!

Winds blew with gale force.

Soldiers with no shoes struggled barefoot in the snow and ice.

Bloody footprints could be seen in the snow on the ground.

Feet and legs froze until the turned black and were amputated.

Morale was at an all time low.

More than 3,000 patriots died that winter.

Men had no blankets to wrap around their bodies while trying to sleep.

Nor did many have clothing to cover their bare bodies.

Defeat and surrender were staring Washington in the face.

Nevertheless, a great number of people believe that God chose this time of misery to give a prophetic vision to George Washington. The story of this remarkable event is fully covered below.

Setting the Scene

There was little hope for victory that day during the winter of 1777. American forces were desperately fighting against the British, at the time the most powerful nation in the world. Did it happen that the great General momentarily dozed and dreamed while sitting in his headquarters at Valley Forge? Or did he have an angelic visit through a daydream? This is the time when George Washington is purported to have had a vision that described the future of the Republic – included were victory in the Revolutionary War; the fighting between Americans in a Civil War; and a World War yet to come.

Yet, great caution must be taken in the acceptance of the validity of any visions or dreams of men. Washington's purported vision, does however, have some quite remarkable factors that seem to be fully factual with regards to U.S. history.

The Origination of the Story

The story of Washington's purported *"vision"* was in the beginning published in the **NATIONAL TRIBUNE** in 1859 and subsequently reprinted in other publications including **THE STARS AND STRIPES**. The *"vision"* was initially described to a reporter named Wesley Bradshaw by an officer (Anthony Sherman) who claims to have served under General Washington at Valley Forge during the winter of 1777.

How it All Began

Mr. Bradshaw begins: *"The last time I ever saw Anthony Sherman was on the Fourth of July, 1859, in Independence Square. He was then 99 years old, and becoming very feeble. But though so old, his dimming eyes rekindled as he gazed upon Independence Hall, which he had come to visit once more."*

"Let's go into the hall," said Mr. Sherman. *"I want to tell you of an incident of Washington's life, one which no one alive knows of except myself; and if you live, you will before long see it verified. Mark the prediction, you will see it verified."*

Washington's Vision as Described by Anthony Sherman

"From the opening of the Revolution we experienced all phases of fortune," reveals Mr. Sherman, *"now good and now ill, one time victorious and another conquered. The darkest period we had, I think, was when Washington after several reverses, retreated to Valley Forge, where he resolved to pass the winter of 1777.*

"Ah! I have often seen the tears coursing down our dear commander's care-worn cheeks, as he would be conversing with a confidential officer

about the condition of his poor soldiers. You have doubtless heard the story of Washington's going to the thicket to pray. Well, it was not only true, but he used often to pray in secret for aid and comfort. And God brought us safely through the darkest days of tribulation.

"One day, I remember it well, the chilly winds whistled through the leafless trees, though the sky was cloudless and the sun shone brightly. He remained in his quarters nearly all the afternoon, alone. When he came out I noticed that his face was a shade paler than usual, and there seemed to be something on his mind of more than ordinary importance. Returning just after dark, he dispatched an orderly to the quarters of an office, who was presently in attendance. After a preliminary conversation of about half an hour, Washington, gazing upon his companion with that strange look of dignity that he alone could command, said to the latter:

Washington Describes His Guests

"I do not know whether it is going to the anxiety of my mind, or what, but this afternoon, as I was sitting at this table engaged in preparing a dispatch, something in the apartment seemed to disturb me. Looking up, I beheld standing opposite me a singularly beautiful being. So astonished was I, for I had given strict orders not to be disturbed that it was some moments before I found language to inquire the cause of the visit. A second, a third, and even a fourth time did I repeat the question, but received no answer from my mysterious visitor except a slight raising of the eyes.

"By this time I felt strange sensations spreading over me. I would have risen but the

riveted gaze of the being before me rendered volition impossible. I assayed once more to speak, but my tongue had become useless, as if paralyzed. A new influence, mysterious, potent, irresistible, took possession of me. All I could do was to gaze steadily, vacantly at my unknown visitor.

"Gradually the surrounding atmosphere seemed to fill with sensation, and grew luminous. Everything about me seemed to rarefy, the mysterious visitor also becoming more airy and yet more distinct to my eyes than before. I began to feel as one dying, or rather to experience the sensations which I have sometimes imagined accompanied death. I did not think, I did not reason, I did not move. All were alike impossible. I was only conscious of gazing fixedly, vacantly, at my companion.

British Defeat Foretold?

*"Presently I heard a voice saying, **'Son of the Republic, look and learn,'** while at the same time my visitor extended an arm eastward.*

"I now beheld a heavy white vapor at some distance rising fold upon fold. This gradually dissipated, and I looked upon a strange scene. Before me lay, spread out in one vast plain, all the countries of the world, Europe, Asia, Africa, and America. I saw rolling and tossing between Europe

and America the billows of the Atlantic, and between Asia and America lay the Pacific.

"'Son of the Republic,' said the same mysterious voice as before, 'look and learn.'

"At that moment I beheld a dark, shadowy being, like an angel, standing, or rather floating in mid-air, between Europe and America. Dipping water out of the ocean in the hollow of each hand, he sprinkled some upon America with his right hand, while with his left he cast some over Europe. Immediately a cloud arose from these countries, and joined in mid ocean. For awhile it seemed stationary, and then it moved slowly westward, until it enveloped America in its murky folds. Sharp flashes of lightening gleamed through it at intervals, and I heard the smothered groans and cries of the American people.

"A second time the angel dipped from the ocean and sprinkled it out as before. The dark cloud was then drawn back to the ocean, in whose billows it sank from view.

Civil War Predicted?

"A third time I heard the mysterious visitor saying, 'Son of the Republic, look and learn.'

"I cast my eyes upon America and beheld villages and towns and cities springing up one after another until the whole land from the Atlantic to the

Pacific was dotted with them. Again, I heard the mysterious voice say, **'Son of the Republic, the end of the century cometh, look and learn.'**

"And this time the dark shadowy angel turned his face southward. From Africa I saw an ill-omened specter approach our land. It flitted slowly and heavily over every town and city of the latter. The inhabitants presently set themselves in battle array against each other. As I continued looking, I saw a bright angel on whose brow rested a crown of light, on which was traced the word **'Union.'** He was bearing the American flag. He placed the flag between the divided nation and said, **'remember, ye are brethren.'**

Reuniting of the North and South?

"Instantly, the inhabitants, casting down their weapons, became friends once more and united around the National Standard.

A World War Foreseen?

"Again, I heard the mysterious voice saying, **'Son of the republic, look and learn.'** At this the dark, shadowy angel placed a trumpet to his mouth, and blew three distinct blasts; and taking water from the ocean, he sprinkled it upon Europe, Asia, and Africa.

"Then my eyes beheld a fearful scene. From each of these continents arose thick black clouds that were soon joined into one. And through this mass there gleamed a dark red light by which I saw hordes of armed men. These men, moving with the cloud, marched by land and sailed by sea to America, which country was enveloped in the volume of the cloud. And I dimly saw these vast armies devastate the whole country and burn the villages, towns and cities that I had seen springing up.

*"As my ears listened to the thundering of the cannon, clashing of swords, and the shouts and cries of millions in mortal combat, I again heard the mysterious voice saying, **'Son of the Republic, look and learn.'** When this voice had ceased, the dark shadowy angel placed his trumpet once more to his mouth, and blew a long and fearful blast.*

God Aids America?

*"Instantly a light as of a thousand suns shone down from above me, and pierced and broke into fragments the dark cloud which enveloped America. At the same moment the angel upon whose head still shown the word **'Union'** and who bore our national flag in one hand and a sword in the other, descended from the heavens attended by legions of white spirits. these immediately joined the inhabitants of America, who I perceived were well-nigh overcome, but who immediately taking courage*

again, closed up their broken ranks and renewed the battle.

"Again, amid the fearful noise of the conflict I heard the mysterious voice saying, **'Son of the Republic, look and learn.'** *As the voice ceased, the shadowy angel for the last time dipped water from the ocean and sprinkled it upon America. Instantly the dark cloud rolled back, together with the armies it had brought, leaving the inhabitants of the land victorious.*

America's Destiny Revealed?

"Then once more, I beheld the villages, towns, and cities springing up where I had seen them before, while the bright angel, planting the azure standard he had brought in the midst of them, cried with a loud voice: **'While the stars remain, and the heavens send down dew upon the earth, so long shall the Union last.'** *And taking from his brow the crown on which blazoned the word* **'Union'** *he placed it upon the standard while the people kneeling down said,* **'amen.'**

"The scene instantly began to fade and dissolve, and I at last saw nothing but the rising, curling vapor I at first beheld. This also disappeared, and I found myself once more gazing upon the mysterious visitor, who, in the same voice I had heard before, said, **'Son of the Republic, what you have seen is thus interpreted. Three great***

perils will come upon the Republic. The most fearful for her is the third. But the whole world united shall not prevail against her. let every child of the Republic learn to live for his God, his land and Union.'

"With these words the vision vanished, and I started from my seat and felt that I had seen a vision wherein had been shown me the birth, the progress, and the destiny of the United States."

"Such, my friend," the venerable narrator, Anthony Sherman, concluded, *"were the words I heard from Washington's own lips, and America will do well to profit by them."*

Pros and Cons
What Do You Think?

According to one obscure internet source: *"This story, charming as it is, appears to be an old hoax. There is no record of Washington ever relating a tale of such a vision* (not according to Anthony Sherman). *The story surfaced long after his death."* What difference could this possibly make insofar as ascertaining its authenticity?

Furthermore, this same source reports the following; *"Oddly enough, the park rangers at Valley Forge are now forbidden to acknowledge George Washington's words."*

Even if it's true that the park rangers at Valley Forge aren't allowed to discuss the subject, this doesn't mean that the story as related by Mr. Sherman is proven false. It simply means that it can't be verified other than by the word of one man. And therefore, it can't be officially acknowledged as historically accurate beyond question. This is completely understandable.

In an apparent effort to diffuse any real likelihood that Washington could possibly have had such an astounding vision in a dream, the Independence Hall Association says this: *"Washington, while willing to refer to religion in political speeches, was not himself a religious man."*

Not a religious man? Literally hundreds of other sources indicate otherwise. His own words for example. Many of his contemporaries also speak of Washington's faith. Read his daughter's letter regarding her father and his religious beliefs and practices in Chapter 2.

The same source unequivocally declares: *"Despite the story being a fraud, it is an old fraud and an historically significant one."*

Yet, they offer nothing further to substantiate their charge of *"fraud."*

Why?

Because there is absolutely nothing to support such a conclusion!

Some people will say that General Washington's vision is validated by the fact that a copy of the account is in the Library of Congress. This argument of authenticity is misleading in and of itself. The Library of Congress has copies of *anything* and everything published in America. This *doesn't* in any manner indicate truthfulness of the content.

I'm not aware of any eighteenth-century evidence that corroborates this story. The soldier mentioned as having a first-hand account of the *"Vision,"* Anthony Sherman, *was* a soldier in the Continental Army. However, according to his pension application, he was at Saratoga under the command of Benedict Arnold at the end of 1777. He is believed to have joined the main forces in 1778 just before the Battle of Monmouth, New Jersey.

Nevertheless, Dr. John Grady, nationally known author, speaker, and patriot, as well as being my friend, offers this: *"As the prophets of old were shown the destiny of mankind, so was Washington shown the destiny of our nation.*

"God molded, inspired and directed George Washington.

"He was, indeed, chosen to be a special man,

"At a special time,

"For a special purpose."

5

Dreams and their Validity

Dreams and the Bible

The **Bible** is filled with a multitude of excellent dream data – both in the **Old** and the **New Testaments**. Throughout the entire Bible there is abundant evidence of a belief in the supernatural origin of dreams. It was an accepted and honored means of communication between the Deity and his chosen ones, for it is written: *"I will pour out my Spirit upon all flesh; and your sons and daughters shall prophesy, your old men shall dream dreams, and your young men shall see visions."*

The Old Testament and Dreams

The best-known dreams of the **Old Testament** are those of Daniel, Jacob, and Joseph. Some authorities claim that the Book of Daniel was written from a dream.

The **Book of Daniel** contains a number of prophetic dreams that were fulfilled to the letter:

The insanity of Nebuchadnezzar and his downfall were presaged.

So was the eventual overthrow of the despotic Balthazar.

Jacob was a man who had many dreams. His dream of the celestial ladder uniting heaven and earth constitutes one of the most beautiful passages in **Genesis.**

His father-in-law, Laban, was warned in a dream that he must not harm Jacob.

In another instance, a distressed King Saul cries out, *"God is departed from me, and answereth me no more, neither by prophets, nor by dreams."*

Dream of the Famine

Joseph, the son of Jacob, was widely known as the "dreamer." While he was in Egypt and working for the pharaoh, the Egyptian monarch had the famous prophetic dream of the fat and lean cattle. Joseph interpreted this dream as a warning of a coming famine. He said: *"God hath shewed pharaoh what he is about to do."*

This dream is credited with saving Egypt from famine and Joseph was aptly rewarded by being appointed chief advisor to the king. The birth of Jesus Christ was also foretold to Joseph in one of his many dreams.

The New Testament and Dreams

Dreams can be found playing an important role as warnings throughout the **New Testament**. For example, The Holy Family was advised in a dream to go into Egypt.

Pontius Pilate's wife warned him after she had a vivid dream at the time of the crucifixion: *"Have thou nothing to do with that just man: for I have suffered many things this day in a dream because of him!"*

Paul was a man who dreamed with regularity.

Many of the apostles were initially converted to Christianity after experiencing dreams.

A multitude of subsequent saints were strongly influenced by dreams—among them is St. Augustine.

Rome's most educated citizens, as well as those of Athens, devoted much time contemplating and writing about dreams.

Plato contended that there were divine manifestations to the soul during sleep.

Dreams are ascribed a supernatural origin by Homer, The Greek and Roman classics contain numerous descriptions of unusual prophetic dreams.

Dreams Foretelling a Death

Many kings and queens have been given warnings of impending danger through a dream:

Caesar, on the night before he was murdered, repeatedly experienced the same dream. He saw himself *"soaring above the clouds on wings"* and placing his *"hand within the right hand of Jove."*

Caesar's wife also had a terrifying dream of her husband being murdered. This took place while she slept during the evening prior to his assassination. She tried to warn the emperor of impending danger.

The Murder of Cassisus of Parma

Cassius of Parma, a supporter of Mark Anthony in a political power struggle, fled Rome and hid in Athens after the difficult battle of Actium. He was sleeping one night and envisioned a tall man who snarled: *"I am your evil genius."*

The apparition appeared again and again in his dreams, always saying exactly the same thing. Early the next morning, he was brutally murdered by order of Emperor Augustus.

Cicero and Dreams

Cicero writes of two traveling Acadians who visited the city of Megara. One went to stay with friends, the other got a room at a local inn. The man who lodged with his friends had a shattering dream that his traveling companion was calling out to him for assistance. The innkeeper was going to kill the man. The dreamer awoke in a sweat, brushed off the horrible dream as nonsense, and proceeded to go back to sleep.

Marcus Tullius Cicero

Wise men are instructed by reason; men of less understanding, by experience; the most ignorant, by necessity; the beasts, by nature.
(106 BCE - 43 BCE)

His friend at the inn appeared in still another dream, this time to tell him it was now too late. He said he had already been murdered, his body tossed in a wooden cart, and covered with dung. Lastly, he revealed that his murderer would try to sneak his body out of town the very next morning. The dreamer now quickly got up, went to see the local authorities, and had the cart searched. The dead body of his friend was easily located and the killer was brought to justice.

The Emperor Marcian dreamed that he saw the bow of the Hunnish conqueror break. This took place on the same night Attila met his death.

Plutarch reveals how Augustus, while sick, was persuaded he should leave his tent after being told of a dream's prophetic warning by a close friend. A few short hours later, his enemies moved in and the bed on which Augustus had slept was pierced by many swords. Heeding a friend's dream saved this leader's life.

Croesus witnessed his son being killed in a dream. And Petrarch clearly talked to his beloved Laura in a dream on the day she died. This dream was the inspiration for his lovely poem, *"The Triumph of Death."*

The distinguished violinist, Tartini, composed the *"Devil's Sonata"* after having a most unusual dream. According to Tartini, he was challenged to a contest of playing skills while having a dream. When he awoke, the music was burned into his mind. He easily committed the entire composition to paper.

Lincoln's Dream of His Death

President Abraham Lincoln and his wife were spending part of a quiet afternoon visiting with friends in the White House. It was Good Friday, April 14, 1865. He described a haunting dream he had recently experienced:

"About ten days ago I retired very late. . . I soon began to dream. There seemed to be a deathlike stillness about me. Then I heard subdued sobs as if a number of people were weeping. I thought I had left my bed and wandered downstairs. There the silence was broken by the same pitiful

Joan of Arc foresaw her own death in one of
her dreams.

sobbing, but the mourners were invisible. I went from room to room. No living person was in sight, but the same mournful sounds of distress met me as I passed along. Every object was familiar to me, but nowhere could I see the people who were grieving as though their hearts would break. I was puzzled and alarmed. Determined to find the cause of a state of things so mysterious and so shocking, I kept on until I arrived at the East Room. There I met with a sickening surprise. Before me was a catafalque, on which rested a corpse wrapped in funeral vestments. Around it were stationed soldiers who were acting as guards; and there was a throng of people, some gazing mournfully at the corpse, whose face was covered, others weeping pitifully.

"Who is dead in the White House? I demanded of one of the soldiers.

"The President, was his answer. He was killed by an assassin.

"Then came a loud burst of grief from the crowd, which awoke me from my dream. It is only a dream but it has strangely annoyed me, however. Let us say no more about it."

That very evening, while sitting in the State Box at Ford's Theater, attending the evening performance of **"Our American Cousin,"** the President was shot by John Wilkes Booth. He died the next day, April 15, 1865.

Index